T0209145

COLLECTION
of
EXPERIENCES
of
EARLY
and
TEEN LIFE
STORIES

With Your Eyes Wide Open
Come Alive

PATRICIA AVILA

WESTBOW
PRESS®
A DIVISION OF THOMAS NELSON
& ZONDERVAN

WestBow Press books may be ordered through booksellers or by contacting:

WestBow Press
A Division of Thomas Nelson & Zondervan
1663 Liberty Drive
Bloomington, IN 47403
www.westbowpress.com
1 (866) 928-1240

Because of the dynamic nature of the Internet, any web addresses or
links contained in this book may have changed since publication and
may no longer be valid. The views expressed in this work are solely those
of the author and do not necessarily reflect the views of the publisher,
and the publisher hereby disclaims any responsibility for them.

Any people depicted in stock imagery provided by Getty Images are
models, and such images are being used for illustrative purposes only.
Certain stock imagery © Getty Images.

ISBN: 978-1-9736-9449-6 (sc)
ISBN: 978-1-9736-9448-9 (e)

Print information available on the last page.

WestBow Press rev. date: 7/13/2020

Life's blessings and of humanity

gift of compassionate

Hoping that the student's simplicity of their childlike innocence and giving them and preparing to show human kindness and to show and reflect the emotions towards those in need. One day form student search and found me and said, I am glad you listened to me about working with the children of Mexican heritage. We need more people like you which I know there are for all diversity for cultures the children have a chance to succeed for their future!

As the day started, I recalled the past experiences with lives that have the challenges for those young lives, that life crossed our paths to experience the daily adventures. Show empathy and compassion for families and individuals with the struggles at their early lives; during the struggles with physical or emotional challenges at their early lives at the time of their school years. So, as with saying from Bremen "With your eyes wide open come alive." As you read there will be some quotation from other respectful compassionated writers.

My first encounter was a child name Dan eight years old in the third grade along having physical challenges along being in a wheelchair bond and was aware of his surroundings. Family wanted more interaction for the child in general education. Ms. Maxwell the third-grade teacher and I would demonstrate with our actions with Dan in the classroom setting by showing as a whole class to participate and interact. Hoping that the student's simplicity of their childlike innocence and giving themselves and preparing to show human kindness. To show and reflect the emotions towards those in need.

At first the rest of the third-grade students weren't sure with the classroom environment and have nothing to do with the student that was different from them. As the year processed slowly the student's awareness of participating with Dan was increasing socializing in the classroom. Each student would read to Dan or ask if he could sit closer to their group table.

The school was able to get a grant for their students with physical challenges and cognitive for a playground and challenge the other students to excel in socializing, develop cognitive growth skills environment. As the year past and slowly the socializing with Dan and the other students from his class was developing between them. So, to beat one unkind act is in kind act a day! "If your answer is "no" then making it mean something. When you stand by your word God will stand by you."

The following year was working with kindergarten students but has challenges for each student. First, there was a small frame thin girl which was not able to talk and didn't respond to socializing. Sure, made it to have one to one care Ben can came from Korea Kane has autism and mom would always carry him Piggy Bank everywhere. Angie always would throw items and didn't feel she didn't need to pick up but eventually by the end of the year. Parents were happy to see her daughter to be responsible and not throwing things and putting items back where she was done playing. Also, Kane learn to walk beside his parents instead of being carried around. Before the end of the year I learned that Kane's mother culture was to carry their children this way but notice that parents learned that it wasn't helping their son. Each year had different students and teachers that worked with this profession. This passage is a sad when because I learned that a student Omari unfortunately was failed by the system because he was not taken away from an unsaved home life environment and lost his life. Then there is David he was quiet and Louise their comfort for speaking with Spanish but with time felt comfortable speaking English later into the year Hannah was from Mexico and her parents were concerned because she stopped eating and speaking at the time. Rosie ISM on a wheelchair bound, but she was a very energetic and no trouble of letting others know that. At the time Rosie was our first wheelchair student and there was no functional disable restroom for her and this concerned me spoke to the school nurse and she surprised me by telling me that Rosie had to face realty and I responded, there are regulation codes to accommodate for student's needs for a good educational function at school sites, but her response is Rosie lives at a universal community area. Which means poverty community and the needs of these students are not easily accommodate for them, so my time was running out and need to go back to classroom and later spoke the teacher and she agreed it was wrong. I ask Ms. Danzler if there was any other way to fix this situation about the bathroom and between us, we came up with a strategy plan and wrote letters to some administration departments and principle about the issue at hand. Even Rosie asked if she could write a letter too. While waiting for a response we did our usual routine at school. One day some girls were teasing Rosie about her tennis shoes, but Rosie learned to ignore response from peers, but her friend Anna started to learn about to speak up at the right time to others from her friend Rosie. This is really helped Anna because she noticed that her new friend had No Fear during

lunch time. I would eat lunch with the classroom.
Family style and even the boys seem to take part
in having conversation during lunch time period
around midyear a new student enrolled in our class,
but Miss Danzler mentioned that it was going to be
a hard transition for the new student and we will
need to be prepared for anything from the student.
So, the day came when the new student Pablo was
not happy that morning and letting everyone know
it starting throwing everything in his reach while
the teacher Miss Danzler tried to distract him I was
going gathering the rest of the students to get out
of the classroom. The students were in front of me
unfortunate problem was able to get a classroom
chair and threw it towards my direction and I got
hit. Later on, I will grab Louise by his jacket and
show him, but Fortunately Louise was much faster

unzip are and took it off, to my surprise Louise ran towards my direction and wanted to help me get up from the floor after that incident the district transfer Pablo to another program. The principal request all staff to come in earlier Friday for a staff meeting and everyone attended the morning meeting. To our surprise since our compass school site is at a government land site some military service officers were present and started the opening of the meeting. At this conversation we learned that the military is awarding a grant for the building of the new elementary school building, and later at conversation the military officer administrator mentioned my team member and my name, along with our student's name Rosie and it came to the military services administration department office receiving a request from letters received at from this school site, which need some new accommodations. Since it was one of the first elementary school build during the Los Alamos for the military in Albuquerque New Mexico for military families. Along, with accommodations for students with physical challenges. The whole staff applauded with such excitement.

It was close for the school year and there is always a talent show that students would participate in and to our surprise Rosie and Anna entered and sang "Walking on the safe side of the street". Two years past and a new year for school to start, unfortunately I was transferred to work with a college student that just graduated, so since Ms. Sara didn't speak Spanish I would translate for the parents and the teacher about the students work and behavioral during time school. At one time I went to eat out with my husband at a

Mexican restaurant and Zymania's mother worked there and then out of no where I felt a hug around my waist and it was Zymania. Usteda Senor tiena una senora bunita y la queo mucho! Which means sir you have a beautiful woman and I care for her. I smiled at them and thank Zymania and said we'll see each other at school. Mom, said to us that with the information that was shared was very helpful for the family that came from Juárez to Albuquerque to make a better life for themselves. Mom said, that participating in the family program that your wife stays till everyone is gone in the evening and helping out to prepare meals and teaching the children with other staff members to take part of understanding family live in Family Involvement program. Going with families in the school bus to trips like Explore, roller skating and helping my daughter in the folkcoro dance and helping the girls to looks nice in their Mexican dress and helping the only boy that is brave in dancing with the girls in the program.

During the school week myself with other staff members will participate in a program for families to work with families involvement some of the students knew me from there and we would have visit home visits at families places one evening I had a home visit and to my surprise voice was yelling towards my direction telling me to go in the house quickly notice that it was a police officer wrestling with a man to the ground and the parents from school opened the door for me she said this always happens in the neighborhood. At the end of the year principle announced that the school budget was for the upcoming year needed someone to volunteer for transfer. So, since I needed a website that has early intervention with infants for my certification required to work with infants and toddlers so there was an opening for a school to be with pregnant teens and young mothers. I submitted my transfer. It was a new start to work with this young population. I was assigned to work with a team with newborn infants and the young teenage mothers so most of the girls were Spanish speaking students and they were hardly anyone who spoke Spanish this language. By the end of the school year the administrator announced it that some of the students were going for summer school and if there were any staff member that wanted to help out there was a girl with her daughter we got close and when we heard I was willing to participate she asked if I would help her out so I did and learn that she would take the bus to my house and tried to catch another bus to go to school talk to my family and mentioned that I wasn't going to be getting a paycheck from this program so, that students would get this more from her part time job. Monday she arrived to pick up her daughter and was very emotional and asked to come in and rest for my daily routine she calm down and said I'm afraid the father of my child knows where I am I heard that he wants to take me back to Ciudad Juarez, but I was so close with finishing school . So, I said if you want just so that there is little of going back and forth, I will help you with transportation every day. I would pick her up from a small apartment to the end and she would have the mind frame to do her senior courses the time came, and she graduated from high school after that I did not see her and her daughter.

My new assignment this time was at the Manzano High school. To assist a wheelchair bound seventeen-year-old girl name Sara. Sara had long black hair and was able to express herself with facial expression and mom is a very intelligent advocate for her daughter. So, mom would find ways to have her daughter the means to excel in high school. Sara is pleasant and enjoyed being with others.

As time passed and learning new methods for Sara. Second year Sara wanted to learn and use a laptop to communicate. Sara was excited about using the laptop; along with enrolling in an editorial class in general education. At this time, I was a silent helper; So, Sara shined and had personal growth as an individual.

During the spring the high school prom was coming up. Sara would hear other fellow classmates talking about it. We were going through the hallway for the next class period. When one of boys from Sara's class approach us, but he was shy to start a conversation with us. Alex is his name and started to first speak to me; Good morning Mrs. A let me help both of you since we're going the same direction. Notice the happy expression on Sara and said, "that will be a great help I said to him." So, we all walked together down the school's hallway. Alex, "Mrs. A. is it possible I could ask, Sara to the prom?" As, Sara was gazing at my direction. I replied to Alex was "Alex Sara is the one you should ask." They both glanced at each other as Sara started to type on her laptop. Sara's voice from the laptop started to speak and as she typed the voice would say "Thank you"

Alex just listening and just the thought of you asking me is a very kind gesture. May I type my phone number to speak to your parents? Sure, Sara said.

During the weekend; Sara's mom called me and ask me about the prom. Mom said, "Sara is so excited could you tell me something about Alex." I mentioned to mom that he would walk along with us in the hallway and would have a conversation with Sara during the school week. He seems pleasant and compassionated, respectful and always showed concerned about Sara's wellbeing."

Monday came along for the school bus to drop off Sara. Usually mom drops Sara off but this time she rode the school bus. The bus driver hand me a note from mom and showed it to the teacher and to her surprise Sara is riding the bus to school for the remaining year. The teacher asked me if I knew anything about it and my replied was that I was as surprise as she was. The teacher said, "Long as I have known mom's pattern, she would always been transporting Sara to school!" I just smiled and started the routine of the day.

The big day came for the prom dance, but this time mom was nerves about it and talked to the staff. I was asked to be in the meeting and mom asked, "If I could accompany her daughter at the prom dance during the weekend?" It was brought to my attention and my reply "Was it's best for Sara's personal nurse to attend with her, because usually the nurse is with Sara during the weekend." I explained that when I met the nurse one day; Sara was always cheerful with her and the nurse would handle any situation if arose for medical reasons. During all this time Sara was listening to all that is said. I turned to Sara wouldn't that be better for this time since it's your first prom dance and the nurse would know exactly what to do?"

Sara was quite for a while, then she started to type on her laptop, and she replied was "True and she does knowing a great hair stylist to make me look nice!"

Prom weekend came. A new week as started but this time Sara's came on the school bus and the bus driver helped Sara down and handed me the school weekly journal and smiled at me! I took Sara in for breakfast but waited for the teacher to give the school journal, but "she asked me did you get to look inside the journal." I replied that I didn't. Let me help Sara with breakfast; while you're reading the journal. As, I read the message my heart just felt full of happiness for Sara, and I recall a verse at the time, and it goes like this. "As to serve with humanity, Mercy, kindness towards those in need with act of dignity." This is what the message said, "Mrs. Pat with much gratitude these two years have been a great change. My husband and I noticed the growth in our daughter, and I noticed the growth in our daughter Sara. She does not have any fear of challenges that comes to her path and along with the message a picture of the couple Sara and Alex." I almost got tearful but took a deep breath. I said, "Sara would you like to share your picture with the rest of the class?" Sara replied, "Great idea!" This was

Sara's last year graduation was coming in May. So, it was our last year together.

This is quotation which I just think of to keep me going on my work experiences each time and so this is why at times there would include with each life story with challenges to inspire anyone to gather strength within to care in with the challenge moments in these stories.

"Sometimes we are so busy adding up our troubles that we forget to count our blessings."

The next year met the assigned team members, along with the students. This year is for the students to learn the personal life skills, which was a new path with them. I would like to say I appreciated the effort for every person to starve to share the time to improve the quality of life for others.

The students would learn to earn and budgeting their finances, and working with others, following directions from supervisors and learning to follow the public bus schedules, transfers.

At first the three of us started in the classroom in the first semester and later then three of us would start out with the students to experience of being out in working within the community. Later, the semester the teacher would be with others in a classroom setting working on their academics on school grounds.

So, the job site was on a community senior center and bus public transportation was 1.5 miles from the school and the students had to learn to ask for a transfer slip. The students had to learn that there were two buses to go to their job site and if the second bus already went by. To look up on the bus schedule on the bus stop posted on the street.

This was the time when there were no cell phones, just land rudders and public phones to use. 7:30 a.m. was the first public bus and Helen and I took Jr. which he was our gentle giant teenager, Billy would not give eye contact with people. Then the girls Tina liked to be our social person with Down syndrome and Shirley had trouble with mobility and time needed to use a wheelchair. Also, there is Jerome with Down syndrome and always liked to sing the songs from the movie Grease, and Elvis songs.

During this time, we would wait for the second bus. There was a small shopping center close to the bus stop and the students just wanted to window shop, and each student watch to learn track time for the bus.

On their job site the supervisor would have extra breakfast food. So instead of throwing the food; she was kind to let our students have breakfast and would say "You're my best workers!" Time past so quickly and our students transition into their work skills developing well.

It was getting close to the winter holidays and we decided to have a party before the winter break. The three of us pitched in to buy some gifts for the students. The Senior center even had a surprise. With

Helen and the teacher mentioned that my birthday is on December. The surprise was on me! We arrived at the Senior Center and started to clean up the tables with the students. Suddenly, a group of Mariachis musicians walked in with our students singing the "Mexican song estas son Las Mananitas" with the students singing along with them. As I listened our students gave me such a blessing even Billy singing his heart out for my birthday. Tina doing a dance with Shirley! Helen brought a gift from everyone and Ms. Chavez with a birthday cake! But to my surprise Tina and Billy handed me a gift and Billy spoke to me! The day ended and my daughter was so excited, because she won concert tickets and ask it Tina's parents would let her go. I asked her parents and mentioned that I would go with the girls to the concert and take all of them home. Saturday came to go for the concert Tina was so happy that she was able to be at the concert. After the concert we started to walk towards the lobby and notice that it was snowing and Tina loves the snow and that really made her evening.

It was a day of blessings as we were waiting for the second bus. We always did some window shopping, but Billy kept surprising us by telling me about how the students notice that I would look at ascertain vest sweater. He said they learned to put it items for layaway and make payments. Ms. Helen finished the story on how the students wanted to buy it for me. So, I learned with a" grateful heart putting others before yourself, and you can become a leader among others." Holiday came and gone. We started a new school year.

As, time went by and the blossoms are springing from the ground, leaves are sprouting from branches. We returned to our daily school routine and with the public bus driver greeting our students with such joy to us again. Each student received a harmonica and they ask the bus driver if they could play the harmonica in the bus. The bus driver's responses "as long there isn't anyone in the bus. But once someone gets in it needs to stop. Helen and I were so surprise and whispered to each other. Hope the students understand what is expected from them, so we thought of the quite game during our bus for our students. Let's see who the first quite one is and who stays quite when people get on board the bus!" It worked!

One day our supervisor mentioned to the staff to start listing names of the students that are prepared to do public transportation on their own. Mr. Moss mentioned that we have some students. The day came and Billy and JR. were the students for this task. So, I was following the public bus with some distances between my car and the bus. "We invest the scared with special importance; we set it aside, and then we believe in it. Graced with our self-imposed halo, we have sometimes miracles flow from it, and as a result miracles flow from it. Since we are always in search of what is special, we tend to bypass the daily marvels of our lives." The following day at the worksite the department's carpenter mentioned that he has a new project for Billy and JR. Which was to fix an antique wheel chair to be auction to the highest bitter. The boys were so proud with how the wheel chair look and within a month the auction started with other items, but to our surprise the wheel chair was the highest prize item.

As time went by and the blossoms are springing from the ground leaves are sprouting from the branches restart it to our daily school routine with the bus driver greeting our students using the public bus each student. At Christmas each student received a hand harmonica and so they each entered the bus ask if they could play their harmonica bus drivers smiled and with grin replied Only while there are no other passengers on the public bus when as soon as you see them getting on board. You need to stop playing the harmonicas, Helen And I was surprised and so after we said It's like playing the quiet game whispering to the students. Let's see who is the quietest one and who stays quiet when the bus stopped, we were surprised everyone stop playing the harmonica. Everyone will get a surprise it worked!

Her supervisor mentioned too Mister Moss the teacher it is time for a student in your classroom is ready to show their life skills they learned with public transportation .the day came and Billy,Jay R where the students for this task and so I was to follow the public bus with my own vehicle. Trying for the students not to notice me following the public's bus but to my surprise Billy Jr. did well in both on bus transportation. At one point when Billy and Jr got off from the bus, they stopped looked around and started looking at the direction I parked my car and looked like they were both laughing pointing at my direction. They sat down on the bus's bench waiting for the second public bus. Mister Moss was waiting at the school site and approached us that there will be a new program and if I was interested in the position to go with the students I am working with right now. So, I applied for the position, which later on I learned that I was picked for working with the same students at Goodwill industries non-profit program with along at-risk students attending Community College.

Another school year ended And I was transferred to another Public school Department this time it was helping out behavioral teens but these students were transferred to finish their education at a Community College we will be attending courses and with a public school teacher at the time miss Hill was to work with myself with guidance for these students. I was a liaison between the public school's teacher and the community professors at the college for the well and success of the of these teenage students.

Some of these students worked at the New Mexico university's student cafeteria and the others would attend Community College courses such as culinary arts Department computers. I would start the week at 5:30 AM in the morning in the culinary cooking classes Hey court time Community College was called TV I and the rest of the students would be at the U.N.M. food court. One time The University students and I missed bus looked had very little time to get back at the turn transition program for the students to board their school bus to go home notice a University college students shutter bugs and approached it with my students ask the bus driver if we could ride with them and mention that we're running late and we will miss their school bus for going home. To my surprise the college students chanted for us to get a ride back to our program best driver asked me where program and told him it was across from where his stop list so he said since it's going my direction he will do it just this one time we think all of them when we were getting off the bus.

The following day was a rainy day most of my students in the culinary baking classes didn't show except one male student this is the time I learned more about this student besides knowing in his school records he was a member local gang, but he really want to change for the better life and would ask for help with the classroom's lesson. So I notice that he was unable to write the notes and struggled, and later when we met at the transition classroom I spoke with the Ms. Hill and advise me for Manuel to use a recorder, but let the professor beware of it before the session started. We both finish our work kitchen I asked him about how he got interested in this field his reply was that he loved cooking with his abuela trying to make good choices for himself because he realized it was just them too then we started our separate ways at the end of the day I got in my car started to head home. When I notice at the bus stop while it was raining and so I parked and approach him. And asked him if you wanted to ride no Senora A. It won't be safe for you where I live. I, said "think of how worried abuela." Consider her feelings And I understood that in his neighborhood wasn't a safe community but who else would do it.

So you finally got in my car and remember he said you're going to stop work I want you to my fear was starting to get to me mad I stayed calm notice some guy standing at the corner St then he said passed by those guys finally arrived at his grandmother's small house he faced me and said besides my abuela believing in me you're a good person I'm going to put every effort to change my life if I had you in kindergarten it might have made a difference after the year I didn't see him in the program with what he said I decided to take a year off to take education courses to be certified in early childhood education. When my year was over I resume working in a public schools started in elementary in bilingual kindergarten classes assisting the teachers in transitioning students which some were students with challenges in general education one day while I was walking to my car I heard I was being addressed Senora A. looked around in spot it an officer standing in the parking lot he approached me and said don't you Remember me. No, I'm sorry I, said I'm one of your former students at the time at the Community College and, "Boy you're hard to track but one of your former colleagues finally gave me the information. I, said "are you Manuel attended culinary arts?" What happened you didn't finish the courses Senora Avila my former gang was trying to force me to go back, but I needed to take care of my grandmother took her out from the neighborhood from harm we moved to Colorado And stayed with some friends which they were kind enough to have my grandmother well I enlisted in the Air Force and continued my education sending money for my grandmother and while I'm still in the service my grandmother and friends open a Mexican restaurant

I enjoy being a cook in the service. And I did get my culinary arts degree I'm very proud and glad that you were able to achieve that Manual, but must say I wondered about your fate said noticed you listen to my words and working with our children of Mexican heritage with People like you which I know there are more people of all diverse cultures the children's have a chance to succeed. Manual left me speechless and so we parted our ways.

As I walked away and got in my car and sat in remembering this verse to give every child the opportunity to have a life of dignity, hope, love especially those with being exposed with physical mental challenges and experience is not being wanted in a family setting with having others to spark a strong faith in themselves to succeed in life's challenges .

ABOUT THE AUTHOR

I am from El Paso, Texas moved with my family to New Mexico, Land of Enchanted. Been living here thirty years with my family.

I first started writing notes about my first grandson and wanted to get others reactions from public library on Storybird. While working at Albuquerque public schools. I am ready to start next adventure with my third book.

Printed in the United States
By Bookmasters